Start TO Finish

FROM Leather TO Football

ROBIN NELSON

LERNER PUBLICATIONS · Minneapolis

Lerner Publications Company
A division of Lerner Publishing Group, Inc.
241 First Avenue North
Minneapolis, MN 55401 USA

For reading levels and more information, look up this title at www.lernerbooks.com.

Library of Congress Cataloging-in-Publication Data

Nelson, Robin, 1971– author.
From leather to football / by Robin Nelson.
    pages   cm. — (Start to finish. Sports gear)
  Includes index.
  ISBN 978–1–4677–3890–3 (lib. bdg. : alk. paper)
  ISBN 978–1–4677–4741–7 (eb pdf)
  1. Footballs—Juvenile literature. 2. Balls (Sporting goods)—Juvenile literature. I. Title.
GV749.B34N45 2015
688.7'633—dc23   2013050213

Manufactured in the United States of America
2-44105-16005-4/28/2017

TABLE OF Contents

Touchdown!

How are footballs made?

First, a worker cuts the leather.

Footballs are made out of leather. A worker cuts out almond-shaped panels with a metal cutter. A machine helps press the cutter into the leather. Four panels make one football.

Next, a machine stamps the panels.

A machine stamps the panels with company logos. It may also stamp the name of a football team or a game, such as the Super Bowl.

7

The panels are weighed.

Each football panel must weigh the same and be the same thickness. A machine shaves extra leather off some panels so they are all the same.

Then a lining is added.

A worker sews a lining onto the back of each panel. The lining makes the football stronger. Then holes are punched where the valve and the laces will be added later.

Next, a worker sews the panels.

A worker uses a sewing machine to sew all four panels together. The football is sewn together inside out. The edges with lace holes are left open.

A worker turns the ball right side out.

The hardest job in a football factory is turning the football right side out. A worker called a turner **steams** the football to make it softer. But the leather is still very tough. The turner uses a pole to turn the football. This takes a lot of strength.

Then a worker adds the bladder.

A bladder holds the air inside the football. A worker puts an empty bladder inside the football. Each bladder has a valve. The valve is pushed through a hole in the football.

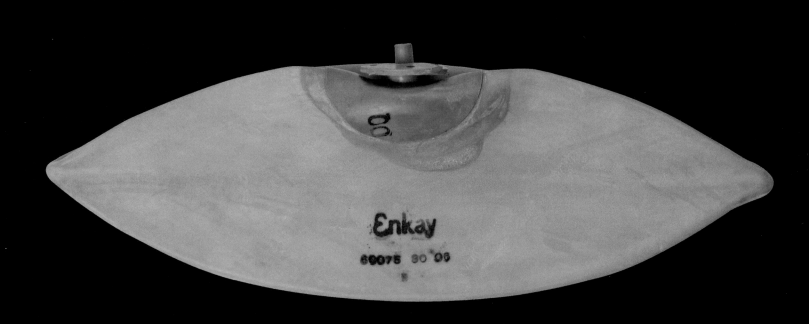

Next, a worker laces the football.

Some air is pumped into the football. Then the lacer uses a tool to pull white laces through the lace holes. This closes the football.

Finally, the football is inflated.

The finished football is put into a mold. The mold gives the ball the perfect shape. Air is added to the football. Then the ball is checked to make sure it is the right size and weight. It's ready for a game!

Glossary

bladder: a balloon-like, air-filled bag inside a ball

inflated: filled with air

laces: cords or strings used for tying or holding things together

leather: a material made out of animal skin

lining: a material that covers an item's inner surface

logos: symbols used to identify a company or a team

mold: a container that gives shape to something

panels: pieces of material that are part of a larger surface

steams: heats something with boiled water that has turned into a gas

valve: a device that controls the flow of air in and out of a ball

Further Information

Jacobs, Greg. *The Everything Kids' Football Book.* Avon, MA: Adams Media, 2010. This book is filled with the latest stats, tackle-worthy trivia, and fun puzzles.

Nelson, Robin. *Football Is Fun!* Minneapolis: Lerner Publications, 2014. Learn football basics including equipment, rules, and how to play the game.

Wheeler, Lisa. *Dino-Football.* Minneapolis: Carolrhoda Picture Books, 2012. See what happens when a group of meat-eating dinosaurs gets together with a group of plant-eating dinosaurs for a friendly game of football.

Where Super Bowl Footballs Are Made
http://money.cnn.com/video/smallbusiness/2013/01/30/smb-where-super
-bowl-footballs-are-made.cnnmoney
See how Super Bowl game balls are made at the Wilson Football factory in Ada, Ohio.

The Wilson Football Factory
http://www.wilson.com/en-us/football/nfl/wilson-and-the-nfl/factory
Tour the factory of the official football of the NFL.

Index

Photo Acknowledgments

The images in this book are used with the permission of:
© iStockphoto.com/Agenturfotograf, p. 1; © Cathy Yeulet/
Hemera/Thinkstock, p. 3; © Amy Sancetta/AP/CORBIS,
p. 5, 13, 15, 19; © The Washington Post/Getty Images,
p. 7, 9; © Matt Sullivan/Reuters/CORBIS, p. 11; © Madison
Sport, p. 17; © Jay LaPrete/CORBIS, p. 21.

Front Cover: © iStockphoto.com/AnthiaCumming

Main body text set in Arta Std Book 20/26.
Typeface provided by International Typeface Corp.